Thanks to Dan Baum, Roy Blount Jr., Vicky Kemp and Avis Meyer, who vetted some or all of my limericks and helped make this a better collection; to Daniel Durchholz, for the book title; to Mark Fowler, for digital dusting; and to Jacob Smullyan, for stepping forward to publish this unlikely project.

This book is dedicated to my parents, Mary Kay and A.S. McDermott.

Foreword

As a teen-aged codger* I composed rags. I'd like to say I enjoyed the challenge of writing in an older style, but in fact, I grew up with and have always loved ragtime. I soon realized the fun with playing with people's expectations, setting them up for 1905, then throwing a curveball from, say, 1940 or 1970. As my tastes expanded, I repeated the process with habaneras, valse-musettes and choros.

Sometime pre-Katrina I started attending a weekly Monday Red Beans and Rice potluck (a New Orleans tradition). One time, I answered the weekly email announcement with a limerick. And thus Beans Lit was born, or so I recall. Others chipped in with their own limericks, haikus, sonnets. I've looked and can't find any of them.

In March 2016 as a middle-aged codger I started spitting out and posting limericks online. The response was hearty and by year's end I had over 200. Historically, limericks have been filthy, but as I kept writing, I thought: "Why not plaintive limericks? Or ones about Claude Monet or Louis Armstrong?" Once Jacob Smullyan of Sagging Meniscus entered the frame, I began illustrating them. And towards

---

*British: codgre

the end of the cycle, I realized, "Oh, I have these drawings I've done over the years, I'll attach limericks to them."

At some point late in the process I realized two things: these limericks were a new creative outlet that I followed because I somehow realized my world of music composition was not expanding in a formal way. Secondly, many of these are little personal nursery rhymes that give me solace in these difficult days.

I will look back at this book—I hope—many years from now, and recognize my life in 2016: two trips to Europe, the love/hate (love more than hate) affair with New Orleans, bemusement towards female/male relations, the loony election.

But right now, I think I'll eat some red beans. It's always food or music in New Orleans.

Tom McDermott
November 2016

Five Lines No Waiting

When limerick-writing be sure
to keep your beat-stressing secure.
    Limit your losses;
    faulty emPHAsis
could render your writing obscure.

Descartes, that thinker sublime,
penned limericks all of the time.
    He made rhyming patter
    the heart of the matter:
"I think, therefore I will rhyme."

For reasons you'd never expect,
Ron loved one synthetic effect.
    His writing's obtuse?
    There was an excuse:
he'd blame it on autocorrect.

You don't have to be an ol' Limey
to learn to use words like, "Oh Blimey!"
    Brit talk is fun,
    and when you are done
you'll sling a slang less five-and-dimey.

In English our cats can be fat;
we mutter the phrase, "dirty rat."
    But because it's so small,
    we don't bother at all
with the unmodifiable gnat.

A mathematician divine
by tweaking an ancient cosine
    quantified pleasure
    and spoke of this measure:
"The pleasure is 7/8ths mine."

She'd begun to abandon all hope,
circling around like a dope.
    Saying to her chauffeur,
    "Cuh-LIE-uh-pee, sir,"
when we all know that it's "Cal-ee-OPE."

There once was a lassie named Urca,
who always went out in a burka.
    She'd dance the fandango
    and tear up a tango
but couldn't pull off a mazurka.

One day the blues shouter Ma Rainey
devolved into VP Dick Cheney.
    The audience stared,
    and really got scared.
Ma thought, "How did my life get so zany?"

I queried a colleague who knows art,
and movies, music and prose art,
    "Who's greatest of all
    in mankind's long haul?
Is it Larry, Curly or Mozart?"

For Louis Armstrong

Hats off to the gent we call "Louie,"
who made the old guard go "Kablooey."
    He conjured new rhythm
    and took the world with 'im.
We don't really doubt this now, do we?

I once spent a night in old Rio;
the music was rootsy, not "neo."
    We dallied till dawn;
    when the gringos were gone
the sambista got lewd with her trio.

In Brazil they have "Rodas de Choro."
It's something that *eu adoro.**
    Passing the scene,
    my attention is keen:
uma coisa que nunca ignoro.

*eu: *ay-oo*

It's almost a portraitist's law:
Eyeballs are tricky to draw.
    But if you can capture
    a cat in mid-rapture
you sidestep this troublesome flaw.

When playing for children, be choosy;
don't lose them with tunes by Debussy.
    If it's not on TV
    they're bored easily,
so hit 'em with "Linus and Lucy."

The groom was a cheapskate, perhaps,
and paid the band nothing but scraps.
    He thought it was frugal
    to book just a bugle;
as revenge he got nothing but "Taps."

For Beethoven

When Ludwig came onto the scene,
musicians all worked for the queen
    or the king or the pope
    or some other dope.
He freed us, you know what I mean?

The German composer Kurt Weill
wrote music that's always in style.
    This music was newish,
    but since he was Jewish
er ging vor dem ersten "Sieg Heil."

Kurt worked in the arts high and low,
amassing a nice pile of dough.
    Yet despite a rich life
    his tune, "Mack the Knife"
is the only one most people know.

At night Fred would drink his martini
and put on some soothing Puccini.
    He did this alone
    because he was prone
to dress in his sister's bikini.

I witnessed the Count Basie Band.
'Twas fearsome, down to a man.
    It made the room shake
    so hard that they'd make
a Muslim drop his Qu'ran.

Since opting to start my own band,
I've trademarked the combo "Tom &."
    This streamlines my style,
    garners some guile
and a chic, gluten-free ampersand.

"Rough!" was one critic's objection,
muttered with deep disaffection.
    Viewers may quibble
    over this scribble;
me? It's a fond recollection.

ODE TO THE ROAD

I can't really find the right grammar,
to channel the joy! The glamour!
    You must use restraint
    or else you will faint,
quite overcome by the clamor.

A young Jewish bride named Amelia
requested a "Hava Nagilia."
    My playing was dreck;
    the hora, a wreck.
"Oy vey," said her bubbe, "I feel ya."

Tom was bopping along, quite carefree
on a devil-may-care keyboard spree.
    He felt quite inventive
    but then got attentive
and noticed, "I'm in the wrong key!"

I'm in love with a gal, twenty-four,
stunningly luscious, top-drawer.
    But Tessie's a teaser,
    and me? Just a geezer—
perhaps you've heard this one before.

How awkward to sit on a jet
with people whom you've never met.
    You try to make chat,
      they'll have none of that.
You leave with a pang of regret.

Things are going just great.
I'm down to my ideal weight.
    My work's going well,
    my love life is swell;
and my fantasy life is first-rate.

I met with a sultry muchacha
and attempted a few rounds of "Gotcha!"
    She yelled at me, "¡EEEE;
    yo no comprendí!"
So much for my high hopes for hotcha.

I've something quite odd to confess:
I'm highly excited by chess.
    When the queen mates a king,
    I imagine a fling
and stymie the urge to undress.

I'll never, ever forget
the magical night when we met.
    We ate escargot—
      or was it shad roe?
in Toledo. Or was it Tibet?

"Come here," my new paramour beckoned,
to whisper things dolce, I reckoned.
    "I'll be faithful to thee,
      till we disagree
for even a wee nanosecond."

She said, "If you want to canoodle,
please buy me that miniature poodle.
    Those diamonds, that yacht …"
      and then the guy thought:
"Well, maybe I'll just have some strudel."

She knew of his wild aberrations
and handled his mild degradations.
    She put up with a heap
    from this outlandish creep
but balked at his defenestrations.

She arched a dark eyebrow at me,
it was certainly easy to see.
    A come-hither trick?
    Or subconscious tic?
Hard to tell on this tiny TV.

She wanted to shoot the sh*t,
he wanted a little bit.
    No sh*t was shot,
    no bit was got
and away they both snuck, in a snit.

An original rocker, EP,
was really quite something to see.
    His dancing was pelvic,
    and thoroughly Elvic,
until he became a draftee.

I have a good friend, name of Morris,
who loves a young lady, Ms. Doris.
    She sells piquant flora
    and has a belle, Nora.
Mo can't the see the trees for the florist.

Paul didn't let people pander.
He wanted a mate's utmost candor.
    A potential one, Lucy,
    was more loosey-goosey,
but Paul was a gander-demander.

"She's a person of substance," they spoke,
"Ask her out, you pitiful bloke."
    With a touch of foreboding
    I followed their goading:
the substance turned out to be coke.

For years I was hooked on this lass.
Such beauty and smarts: she had class.
    An affair in the clover?
    Nah, I couldn't get over
a sizable ethnic crevasse.

A beautiful babe was a-wishin'
for attention, and so went a-swishin'
    to the local marina,
    dressed like a czarina,
to try out her compliment-fishin'.

I know a magician quite lewd,
routinely referred to as "rude."
    His abracadabras
    were shockingly scabrous;
delivered, of course, in the nude.

I once had a roommate named Rex
who had only unfiltered sex.
    Just copping a condom
    was simply beyond him;
this led to a thin Rolodex.

I made her a sultry advance,
suggesting we both head to France.
    She said, "I'll take Nice
    and you: head north, please."
A twist in long-distance romance.

We dined on the Peloponnesus
where the knowledge of English decreases.
    We ordered the lamb,
    they brought us cold Spam
in a misguided quest to appease us.

I'm spending a nice time in Hamburg,
a very appealing-to-Tom burg.
    The Reeperbahn's gross,
    and leaves you morose,
but the rest is a nice pop-and-mom burg.

I went to the land of the Swiss
for get-back-to-nature-type bliss.
    I saw moo-cows and bankers
    but no oil tankers,
and I am quite thankful for this.

Heinrich began his subscription
to the magazine, "Ancient Egyptian."
    It's grist for this critic
    of things pyramidic
and similar forms of encryption.

Prague is a polyglot stew.
Millions of people come through:
    folks of all nations,
    Africans, Asians,
and four or five Czech people too.

When Luther set out on his mission
he started a nasty division
    twixt Shi'ite and Sunni
    —oh wait, that's just loony—
I've never been one for precision.

Luther was nixed from the choir
for starting a doctrinal fire.
    Well, that's what you get
    when you go tête-à-tête
with Pope Leo and call him a liar.

Afar, on a mountain, did dwell
a princess, trapped in a cell.
    Her life was severe,
    so each night you'd hear
the piteous bawl of the belle.

I wasn't prepared for his screed
after a minor misdeed.
    My Danish friend Ulf
    went through the roof
just cuz I called him a Swede.

Call a fellow from Sweden a Dane?
It really won't cause him much pain.
    Swedes have the knack
    of being laid-back.
With women like theirs, why complain?

A shooting of two, three or four
made the frothy front pages of yore.
    Now it takes eight
    if Tech's playing State;
for Super Bowl, 15 or more.

In NOLA, good cheer is unchecked.
We parade as you'd never expect.
    Gals take umbrellas
    and wake up their fellas.
It's one more excuse to get wrecked.

My town stresses pleasure, not toil;
there's often a free crawfish boil.
    We've many a swell fish,
    essentially shellfish;
you don't even have to add oil.

The crime rate is presently soaring;
our roads require constant restoring.
    But folks in this town
    pretty much stick aroun';
most anywhere else seems so boring.

Though it took him a lifetime to learn,
a who-dat was pleased to discern
    that when tooling aroun'
    in ol' Nola town
it's lawful to signal a turn.

CITY OF "ASK" MURDERERS

In London you get overtaxed,
while Rio has spas, to get waxed.
    But NOLA's a place
    where people embrace
a reversal: that is, to get "aksed."

Whenever the Saints fall apart,
it breaks the Orleanian heart.
    We feel bereft
    'cuz all we got left
is music and eating and art.

"I give," claimed our quarterback, Kent,
"A hundred and twenty percent."
    His teammate would strive
    for one hundred five.
Kent clucked, "What an indolent gent!"

Cannibal Bob was no yokel
and could, at times, be very vocal:
    "In almost all cases,
    I shun foreign races
and try really hard to eat local."

The nutter who maintains our quad
is creepy; incredibly odd.
    He's cunning and cruel
    with many a tool;
they call him the Marquis de Sod.

I hired a cleaner named Vic
to make my pad shiny and slick.
    From what I'd observe he
    would clean topsy-turvy,
so things ended up span and spick.

Down at the store for some creamer,
I lo and behold saw a lemur!
    I stood there agape,
    then tried to escape
as he jumped up and down on my femur.

Our localite, Stu, made a stir
presenting his new talking cur.
    The town got all tinglish:
    "He really speaks English??"
Poor Phideaux replied, "Non, monsieur."

Citing a top-secret source,
a pig told me something quite coarse.
    I couldn't conceive it,
    but now, I believe it:
it came from the mouth of a horse.

A Guernsey from west Curaçao
felt like taboo-breaking somehow.
    He wore, for no reason,
    some antlers in season,
and now he's a quite hole-y cow.

An ocelot pilfered my knee,
which started a larcenous spree.
    I felt, frankly, glum;
    my sister went dumb,
cuz the cat got her tongue, don't you see?

Regarding our planet earth's breedahs,
the felines are natural leadahs.
    Chock-full of virtue,
       they won't lie and hurt you
except, it is said, for the cheetahs.

Greg yelled for "Quiet!" when groggy,
and spent some down-time with his froggie.
    Even a "ribbit"
       he'd strictly prohibit;
if it tried it was fed to his doggie.

A moose I met on the loose
was sipping some juniper juice.
    Unlike the White Rhino,
       this boy was albino:
vanilla, not chocolate moose.

Over several extremely nice clarets,
a hare told his sweet of his merits.
    "Marry me, dear,
        I'll provide, don't you fear,
beginning with 24 carrots."

Needing to get in the black,
Dag sold his Jag for a yak.
    He stopped buying gas
        and fed the beast grass;
now it's addicted to crack.

I recently rented a hamster
who was, sad to say, quite a scamster.
    This dastardly dude
        would pilfer my food
and moonlight, at night, as a spamster.

JUDD! THANKS FOR TAKING MY CALL! SO HERE'S THE PITCH: IT'S "SEVEN YEARS IN TIBET" MEETS "SNAKES ON A PLANE": "YAKS ON CRACK!"
..... JUDD?
JUDD??

A chicken and wren, being quirky,
had a trans-genus chat that was murky.
    Said the wren, "What confusion!
    Let's stop this delusion
and simply agree to talk turkey."

What if an object, inert,
became, overnight, self-alert?
    As it glowed on the shelf
    would it ponder itself?
Or shrug and ask, "What's for dessert?"

The moon just swallowed the sun.
America outlawed the gun.
    The earth's proven flat;
    on top of all that,
the Cubbies are now #1.

Shooting my first hole-in-one,
I'm happy with what I have done.
    Smack in the groove,
      how can I improve?
By shooting my first hole-in-none?

Mac and Minnie began to consign
which buddies would join them, to dine.
    She said "Vicky, or Vern?"
      He said, "I've no concern.
Your guest is as good as mine."

The bloke told the owner of Vicken's,
a bookstore with glorious pickin's,
    "Please, 'A Tale of Two,' er …
      wait, my mind's just a blur."
The owner replied, "What, the Dickens?"

Finding my words too prosaic,
I'll now make my curses archaic.
    No more "Gosh darn it!"
    Now it's "Consarn it!"
And soon I'll move on to Hebraic.

This mandolin player was slick,
A cannibal, too, with a shtick.
    He wore grassy skirts
    and—sorry, this hurts—
he oft had a bone, to pick.

My neighbors adopted a stray,
but couldn't, it's funny to say,
    come up with a name.
    They tried, nothing came.
They finally called it a day.

Said my lady-friend Jeanie-Marie,
"A granny's what I want to be."
    Then she thought, with a groan,
    "I've no kids of my own."
A conundrum, I think you'll agree.

A rhinoceros, feeling some scorn,
decided to alter his horn.
    He's feeling less nasty
    with new rhinoplasty,
and now he won't feel so forlorn.

A hipster created a blog
so boring no one left agog.
    "It features my cat;
    it's dull, I see that.
Tomorrow I'll showcase my dog."

An author was writing a farce
but found that the laughs were too sparse.
    Then he crafted a plan:
    he'd have the lead man
repeatedly fall on his arse.

There once was a down-and-out schmo
who became quite a regular joe.
    With schmo-ness removed
    his image improved
and he made some ridiculous dough.

Her sign said, "Five cents for a tickle."
A definite deal for a nickel.
    Things quickly turned prickly
    o'er who was the ticklee
and business slowed down to a trickle.

Monet was a Frenchman renowned
as the most fertile artist around.
    Painting piece after piece
    he vowed not to cease
till his whiskers were brushing the ground.

A curator, under some pressure,
sought artwork that might bring more pleasure.
    She dillied with Dali
    and Gaudi, by golly,
then finally settled on Escher.

People creating for whimsy
garner an income that's flimsy.
    It's not anti-greed,
    but internal need
to keep them from feeling too grim, see?

When Picasso would render your face,
your features he'd often displace.
    You'd sit for a pose,
    get a wildebeest's nose
and smelling salts, too, just in case.

When waking I feel disconnected;
sans coffee I feel disaffected.
    My craving's so vast,
    I need it so fast,
I now gotta have it injected.

His joe took forever to make,
a mocha frappé almond shake.
    Behind him in line
    I don't feel benign:
"Why can't they just let him eat cake?"

Have you ever come out of a dream
and things aren't the way they should seem?
    You're in mystery's thrall
    when you slowly recall
the 23 shots of Jim Beam.

Better to perish from gout?
Or ZAP: "This one's dead, ain't no doubt"?
    One's a painful demise,
    two allows no goodbyes;
seems there's no easy way to check out.

I once knew a Texan named Tina
who laughed like a hopped-up hyena.
    Doctors, stumped by her wheeze,
    parsed her disease:
she'd swallowed a small ocarina.

The feeling we call "dèjá vu"
mixes the old and the new.
    It seems a bit eerie
      and makes us feel leery,
the feeling we call "dèjá vu."

A patient, around 63,
said, "Doctor … what do you see?"
    He replied, "As it stands,
      it's all in my hands.
So don't pray to God, pay to me."

You gotta have one type of "osis?"
Consider some mild halitosis.
    Thrombosis can chill you,
      necrosis can kill you.
Bad breath? Just let folks hold their nosis.

Everything's turning out worse?
Let me please intersperse.
    Smoking's near-vanished,
    indoor's it's banished
in a way sometimes smooth, sometimes terse.

I learned of a fellow who grows hairs,
adding to your these-and-those hairs.
    The bald were encouraged
    but soon were discouraged:
this quack only boosted your nose hairs.

The medic did much to exalt
his new pill, one might say, to a fault.
    "Studies have shown:
    don't take it alone,
you must add a wee grain of salt."

Mr. Crump was a crabby old critter;
brutal and biting and bitter.
    His docs said, "Be nicer;
    at least be conciser,
and vent all that anger on Twitter."

History's not written in stone;
you can't trust just one voice, alone.
    It's fed through a filter
    and might be off-kilter;
leaving facts largely unknown.

It's not done exactly by hook,
nor is it precisely by crook.
    But it's hard to construe
    the things people do
to get their damn names in a book.

They say that Obama's Islamic,
a notion I find rather comic.
    If ever the Prez
    would try on a fez,
Bill O'Reilly would sure go atomic.

Clinton told us, "I gotta regale ya:
stand by me and I'll try not to fail ya.
    I'll master survival
    by letting my rival
obsess on—get this—genitalia."

There once was a real-estate brat
who knew not his butt from his hat.
    He assaulted the misses
    and reeked of Narcissus,
and boy, are we tired of that.

A citizen, one sorta snooty,
decided to shirk jury duty.
    In the juristic pool
      he yelled, "FRY the fool!"
The DA yelled back, "Well, aw rooty!"

Something for which I can vouch:
Gramps was a terrible grouch.
    He'd rant and he'd rave,
      misconstrue, misbehave—
all without leaving the couch.

The fellow right here's my late Pops.
This kinship, of course, never stops.
    I used to dismiss him;
      but now I quite miss him
and give him the fullest of props.

For People Who Can't Draw Teeth

This here's my Mom, Mary Kay.
I think of her most every day.
    This toon's no pure
    mother's likeness for sure;
read on! I have more to relay.

Her pearlies I asked her to hide;
and although she took this in stride,
    there's a palpable grimness
    a hint of false primness
concealing the sweetness inside.

Sherman would keep his mouth shut;
a quirk that could irk you somewhat.
    His patter was gnomic,
    low-key, palindromic.
The worst that he'd curse was "Tut-tut."

Hesitancy was his way,
tense, on the fence, every day.
    He couldn't find rest
    for his feverish breast:
should he hit, say, the sack or the hay?

His speech had a curious cast:
retrospection … left him aghast.
    For him, it made sense
    to shun the past tense.
He'd had an extremely tense past.

The movie star Mario Lanza
sure wasn't a paramahansa.
    He made his peers grieve, "Oh,
        what a big divo,"
but really could belt out a stanza.

A palsie said, "Hey listen, buddy,
your rhyming is way fuddy-duddy.
    Try rhyming arrhythmic;
        you'll have a new githmick
and open a new field of study."

I dreamt of a Persian koala
who couldn't relate much to Allah.
    He tried being Sufi
        but found it too goofy;
he finally took up Kabbalah.

He bought his new wife an impala,
and said that he shelled out top dollah.
    It had hooves and a tail
    and caused her to wail:
"I'm not putting up with this squalah!"

She photographed food for her trade,
and often was quirkily paid.
    "We're strapped," said her bosses,
    "and must cut our losses.
It's Kibbles, not cash, we're afraid."

I was sent into joyful deliria
by emails seeking criteria.
    My passwords, my bank,
    and this was no crank,
but a trustworthy gent from Nigeria.

During some recent cavortin',
this was the hat I was sportin'.
    Sought the "Old Blue Eyes" look;
    instead got mistook
for a less-dapper fella: Ed Norton.

The cowboy was given to prattle
'bout his 10,000-head herd of cattle.
    "They roam by my place,"
    but friends found no trace;
he'd long lived in downtown Seattle.

Old cowboy songs: hard to beat 'em;
cows and how cow wranglers treat 'em.
    They use tender words
    serenading their herds
but no tips on how best to eat 'em.

I have an amigo named Floyd
who's shaped like a trapezoid.
    Though clearly appalled,
    the CIA called
to see how he might be deployed.

Some people find him just frightful;
others think he's so delightful.
    Folks 'cross the aisle
    you think in denial
will not find your comments insightful.

Joe took some puffs on his hookah
and challenged a drunken palooka.
    The crowd was astounded;
    Joe shoulda been pounded
but luckily had a bazooka.

There once was a pilot named Vinny
who really was kind of a ninny.
    He toked in the stirrup
    and took off for Europe
but ended up over New Guinea.

Whenever poor Tex felt too addled,
he prepped his ol' horse to get saddled.
    The horse sensed his mood,
    found it too rude,
got skittish and scared and skedaddled.

Southern accent limerick:

I find that listening to Bach'll
warm my most every cockle.
    But when I play J.S.
    it's really a may-ess.
You might even say a debacle.

Hal hated to give a big pest room,
but finally offered a guest room.
    It featured a futon
    the size of a crouton
and whoa, what a risible restroom!

Adolfo had no clue at all;
his arrogance cast a huge pall.
    A friend said, "You prig!
    Your head's way too big!"
His retort: "No, my hat's way too small!"

Sid said to the man, "Watch it, bub!"
The mobster shot back, "Why you schlub!!"
    Sid got shoes of cement
    for his final descent
and now he goes "GLUB, glub, glub, GLUB."

She had an emotional spasm
that opened a terrible chasm.
    After her fit,
      her Romeo split;
she wonders now which girlfriend has 'im.

When it's frigid, we usually choose
to stay in our bed for a snooze.
    We only go out
      when we look all about
and discover we drank all the booze.

Some things I certainly dread,
but I readily forge ahead.
    I summon up vigor,
      incredible rigor,
and finally get out of my bed.

I'm aching to join the harangue
along with the rest of the gang.
 But a message one day
  said, "Don't join the fray.
It's bad for your yin and your yang."

Sometime around late-middle age,
your friends begin leaving the stage.
 So, for a start,
  you open your heart
and do what you can to engage.

I find that my hopes are ascending,
and my search for a mate might be ending.
 She laughs at my wit,
  or if that isn't it,
she does a great job of pretending.

A haunted house once had a host
who sought to extract the utmost
    cash from consumers
    who'd heard all the rumors,
and told him "don't give up the ghost."

Needing an extracurricular
I sought a task rather vehicular.
    Any dumbbell
    can park parallel;
I wanted to park perpendicular.

A foreman once sought to bestow on
a seamstress some guidance to go on.
    "Please keep alert,
    finish that shirt,
and sew on and sew on and sew on."

When passing down Yiddish to tots,
it's best to connect all the dots.
    I'm certain that it's
    okay if they schvitz,
but don't overdo it: they'll plotz.

SCHVITZ

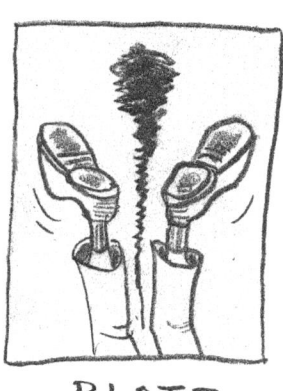

PLOTZ

There once was a Manhattan princess
who ate only raspberry blintzes.
    These left crimson streaks
      on her blue-blooded cheeks,
resulting in shudders and winces.

There lived in Chicago a fogey
who loved an occasional stogie.
    He had a bad cough;
      this did not kill him off.
Instead it was too much pierogi.

Rover is not a delight;
a grumpy ol' greyhound, all right.
    There's nothing to fear
      except for his sneer:
his snark is far worse than his bite.

He handled his every vexation
with over-the-top mastication.
    And since the election
    he's seen his mid-section
defy every known explanation.

North, where the Lakes are called Great,
there's room for aquatic debate.
    One lake's Superior.
    The others: Inferior?
Defective? Lowdown? Second-Rate?

He's a fellow who's so doctrinaire.
All is in place, every hair.
    He's so "every-day,"
    even square people say,
"They sure fixed the mold with Pierre."

Drink: what a true pleasure-giver.
At its best it'll make you just quiver.
    It oils interaction
    with one small distraction:
it also poleaxes your liver.

Irving, our waiter, was serving
clumsily, yes, he was swerving.
    We soon began thinking
    that Irv had been drinking.
In all, it was very un-Irving.

He promised to uphold the law,
but then turned around and said, "Naw!"
    Despite this misdeed
    I paid him no heed
till they came for my Ma and my Pa.

I thought I was wholly alone
in my sad, middle-aged Luddite zone.
    Then I called up a friend
    on whom I depend
because he still answers his phone.

He once was a journalist ace;
covered many a troublesome case.
    But after this phase he
    got rather lazy.
Now he writes for the Book of Face.

He lived with his elderly mother,
three sisters, a dog, and his brother.
    They'd no cash at all,
    and as they'd recall
at best they had only one druther.

There once was a lady named Zsa Zsa
who lived, more or less, like a rajah.
    She danced every numba
    and really could rumba
but never did manage a cha-cha.

Through heaven's mysterious ways,
reward cancels out awful days:
    Negating bronchitis,
    even phlebitis
and ten-hour airport delays.

You peer out from the gig, and you gauge:
are there wimmins to talk to off-stage?
    You see a babe, thirty,
    and think you'll be flirty,
then recall that you're somewhat stone-age.

"Candy is dandy but liquor,"
said funny old Ogden, "is quicker."
    The need seems innate
    to self-medicate
from the reprobate o'er to the vicar.

People use food or cocaine
to stifle their innermost pain.
    What causes this strife?
    Could it be a past life?
Maybe so, if you're Buddhist or Jain.

We must use the power within
instead of resorting to gin.
    And I would contend
    that many lives end
before this advice can sink in.

I turned on some cable TV,
and was soon overwhelmed with ennui.
    200 stations,
        zero temptations.
Just crazy. Or is it just me?

Le garçon was a word prodigy;
bon mots of the highest degree.
    Turns of phrase, aperçus,
        till his friends said, "adieu,"
for he was as mean as could be.

Bea's booty led fellas to smirk;
she needed to tweak her twerk.
    Guys used to giggle
        when she would wiggle:
now they are driven berserk.

I certainly don't own a castle,
nor could you call me a vassal.
    I don't drink or dope;
      the bayou's my hope
to transcend this temporal hassle.

He wanted to go to and fro;
she needed to just do-si-do.
    They took dancing lessons,
        had counseling sessions
and found they had nowhere to go.

Taping some smut on his mobile,
he mused, "This could really go global.
    But I'm no broadcaster;
        in fact, I'm a pastor
who needs to at least appear noble."

There once was a corpulent swami
who couldn't stop eating pastrami.
    He knew the causation:
        oral fixation.
Something to do with his mommy.

Carnival, one could agree,
is an off-and-on decadent spree.
    Now we get ashes,
    but not 40 lashes.
Sounds like a good deal to me.

One morning, 'round quarter-to-four,
Sue's soul let her bod to explore.
    While floating midair,
    it looked here and there,
and sputtered, "We MUST clean this floor."

A schnitzel, a snippet, a sip;
our life now is just one such blip.
    Buddhists will say
    we pack everyday
for the next back-to-planet earth trip.

Limericks can be very plain,
Or somewhat outré if you deign.
    Point-of-view can be formal
    then quickly, abnormal.
"Well, of course, I have visited Spain!"

A car buff, while traveling one day,
was tragically led quite astray.
    He visited Spain
    seeking carros arcane
and wound up at an auto-da-fé.

A boxer had quite a proboscis,
you might even say a colossus.
    When forearms went weak,
    he'd then use his beak
to administer punishing crosses.

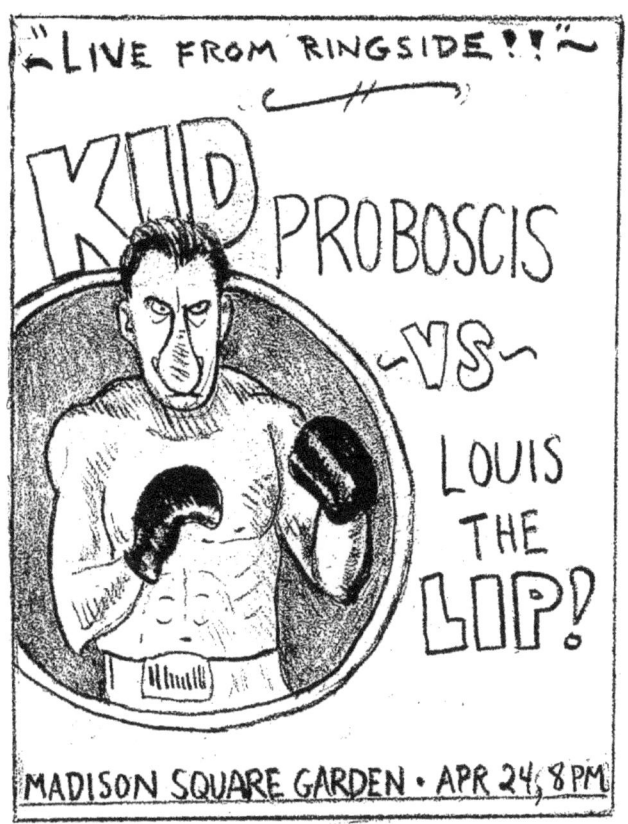

Jim ordered a nice breakfast quiche
that was secretly dosed with hashish.
    By the end of the day
    I'm sorry to say
he had to be walked on a leash.

The elder remarked to the nipper,
"Try your darned best to be chipper.
    Don't lie and cheat,
    watch what you eat
and never date more than one stripper."

There once was a Cuban named Tito
who wanted a presence bonito.
    With new romance looming
    he worked on his grooming
and started to dress all cognito.

Her husband was known for his sleekness,
but then turned to food out of meekness.
    He ate and re-ate
    and gained so lotsa weight.
She's entered him now in the Preakness.

She crafted a a well-crafted tweet
and thought it was pretty darn sweet.
    But something was wrong:
    it was too long.
And so it appeared incom

I know a political lummox
who seems to exist just to flummox.
    He lies, oh, so badly,
    and really quite madly,
until we are sick to our stomachs.

Critters need sounds to romance to,
tunes that are easy to dance to.
    Folks say that elk
    adore Lawrence Welk
because he's so easy to prance to.

Stepping out of the SAS doorway
I'll disembark Tuesday in Norway.
    If I find, in a lurch,
    I must attend church,
I'll worship the Odin-and-Thor way.

Oslo's a city where I'm
spending a wee bit of time.
    Street after street,
    tidy and neat.
But boy it's a tough word to rhyme.

Faces are turning to stone,
aghast at the hurricane zone.
    Catholics are praying,
    Baptists are swaying,
Zen Buddhists make do with a koan.

Since I have some time to piddle,
here's an obit for Y.A. Tittle:
    "Every fall,
    he threw the ball,
and chewed his tobacco spittle."

Nantucket's a word I've not used.
Verily, I stand accused.
    I'd look the fool
    going old school
and Facebook would not be amused.

A hyena walked into a bar
and started his "hardy har har."
    The pub said, "Okay,
      we'll let you stay."
Until he lit up his cigar.

He thought his next gig was in Nashville;
turned out instead it was Asheville.
    He found the mistake
      then said, "Oh God's sake."
And started to act real bashville.

A poor Irish fellow named Flanigan
could only afford one shenanigan.
    One day he reckoned
      he'd save for a second
and act like a good rowdy man again.

Slathered in lime guacamole,
the monk muttered mantras unholy.
    He'd plead and he'd plead,
      "Come follow my creed!"
and supplicants came, but quite slowly.

LOPSIDED LIMERICK

We knew he was ace at debasing
himself, in a phase of disgracing
    himself. Boy he'd drink
    until you might think
"Man, he is really erasing

    _____"

I said to my butt, "Please don't dial.
This phoning is never in style."
    It replied, "C'mon dude,
    I know that it's rude
But I need some fun once in a while."

There once were a coupla wretches
attempting some new yoga stretches.
    Things didn't go well;
    they moaned, "Bloody hell,"
and similar sorts of kvetches.

He thought about saying "P'shaw,"
but pondered a bit and thought, "Naw.
    I'd sound like a snoot;
    So I'll go galoot,
and simply say, 'Haw, haw, haw.' "

Banana slugs don't get the jitters
consuming microbial critters.
    They'll eat a bug
    with nary a shrug
and love protozoa with bitters.

Cat-o-saurs: yes, they're still roaming
in faraway parts of Wyoming.
   I wouldn't bet
     they make a good pet.
Think of the hours of combing.

Her students, they knew how to spell;
but their lexicon wasn't too swell.
    They said, "Teach, this one trips us:
    What's an ellipsis?"
The teacher, Dot, smiled and said, "Well…"

The girlfriend yelled, "Wait a sec!
This new woman from Prague… what the heck?!?"
    He said, "Have no fear,
    I've no interest, dear."
Still, she fears that her male's in the Czech.

The women once threw him their panties,
and similar pieces of scanties.
    As a sexy young thing
    he really could sing.
Now he gets gifts from great-aunties.

Karma caught up with ol' Tim
while biking his way to the gym.
 Because of a past fault
 his ass felt the asphalt.
We hope that's the last spill for him.

He wanted to practice some numbas,
including some difficult rhumbas.
 But up came a thrombus
 shaped like a rhombus.
At present he more or less slumbas.

The wizard said, "You listen now, sir,
I'll hurt you, you wanna know how, sir?"
 The doofus said, "Dare me?
 Go on, you don't scare me!"
and then got turned into a schnauzer.

A connoisseur, sick of Art Deco,
sought something more grave: an El Greco.
    But he settled, by gosh,
    for Hieronymus Bosch:
human torso and head of a gecko.

When a gecko says, "Hey, it's a wrap!"
listen, and don't be a sap.
    So thank you for reading
    but now I'll be needing
a hundred-and-two-hour nap.

If you are a regular joe,
self-portraits aren't easy, you know.
 But if you're among creatures
 with lopsided features
at least expectations are low.

Tom McDermott was born in St. Louis, Missouri in 1957, and moved to New Orleans in 1984. As a pianist/composer he has released 15 CDs. This is his first book. His website is mcdermottmusic.com.

www.ingramcontent.com/pod-product-compliance
Lightning Source LLC
Chambersburg PA
CBHW020944090426
42736CB00010B/1252